In and Out

Out

TEACHING PREPOSITIONS

BY YVONNE PEARSON

The Child's World®
childsworld.com

Published by The Child's World®
1980 Lookout Drive • Mankato, MN 56003-1705
800-599-READ • www.childsworld.com

ACKNOWLEDGMENTS
The Child's World®: Mary Swensen, Publishing Director
Red Line Editorial: Editorial direction and production
The Design Lab: Design

Photographs ©: Jiri Vaclavek/Shutterstock Images, cover (left),
2–3; Emilia Stasiak/Shutterstock Images, cover (right), 1; Africa
Studio/Shutterstock Images, 4–5, 6–7; Hong Vo/Shutterstock
Images, 7; Shutterstock Images, 8, 9, 11; Daria Gulenko/
Shutterstock Images, 10; Ronnachai Palas/Shutterstock Images,
12–13; Gunnar van Eenige/Shutterstock Images, 14–15

ISBN 9781503808379
LCCN 2015958422

Printed in the United States of America
Mankato, MN
June, 2016
PA02304

ABOUT THE AUTHOR
Yvonne Pearson is a poet who loves to play
with words. She also writes essays and books.
She lives in Minneapolis, Minnesota.

A **preposition** is a word that describes how two things relate, usually about direction, place, or time. Look for **prepositions** in this book. You will find them in **bold** type.

Rosa looked **for** her cat **behind** the chair. She did not find her cat.

Rosa looked **under** the sofa. She did not find her cat, but she found a book.

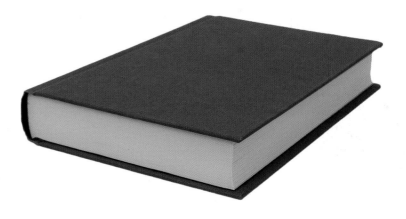

Rosa climbed **up** the steps and lay down **on** her bed. She leaned **over** the edge and looked **beneath** the bed. The only thing there was her cat's toy.

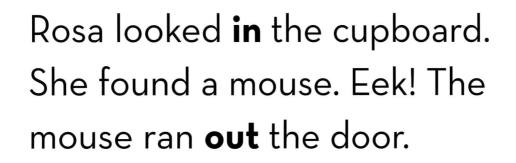

Rosa looked **in** the cupboard. She found a mouse. Eek! The mouse ran **out** the door.

Rosa looked **until** dark. No cat. **After** she went **to** bed, she whispered, "I miss my cat."

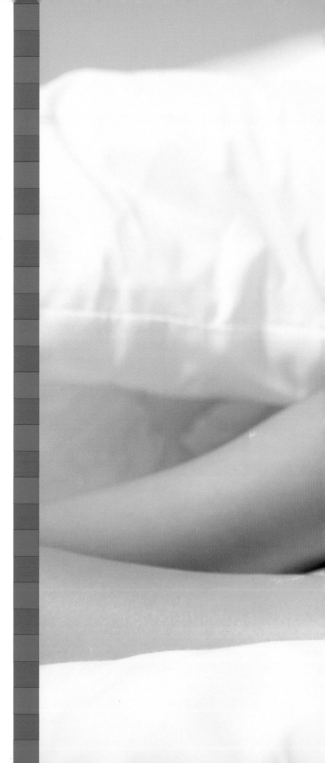

In the morning, Rosa smiled. She found her cat curled **beside** her pillow **on** her bed.

Did you find these prepositions?

after   out
behind   over
beneath   to
beside   under
for   until
in   up
on

To Learn More

IN THE LIBRARY
Ayers, Katherine. *Up, Down, and Around.* Somerville, MA: Candlewick, 2008.

Marsico, Katie. *Prepositions.* Ann Arbor, MI: Cherry Lake, 2013.

Walton, Rick. *Around the House the Fox Chased the Mouse.* Layton, UT: Gibbs Smith, 2011.

ON THE WEB
Visit our Web site for links about prepositions: **childsworld.com/links**

Note to Parents, Teachers, and Librarians: We routinely verify our Web links to make sure they are safe and active sites. So encourage your readers to check them out!